AF480946

This book belongs to

Our NICU Journey

written by
Sarah Immonen Ward

illustrated by
Andrea Brasier

littlewardbooks.com

Written by Sarah Immonen Ward
Illustrated by Andrea Brasier
Book Design by Intricate Designs
Edited by Tamara Rittershaus and Debbie Manber Kupfer

ISBN: 979-8-9851312-1-5 (paperback)
ISBN: 979-8-9851312-0-8 (hardcover)
ISBN: 979-8-9851312-2-2 (ebook)

Library of Congress Number: 2021922474

Thank You!

To my husband Alex: thank you for being my rock on our hardest days and for being a constant source of love and encouragement. I am thankful to have you as my partner in life, and I love you always. To our three miracles Isabelle, Evelyn, and Theodore: as you grow into your own remember to be kind, courageous, and know that you are loved.

To our friends and family who supported us and never lost hope.

To the medical team and staff: without you we would have nothing, but because of you we have everything.

To the Jenkins family: thank you for your courage in sharing your story of loss and victory. Let us always remember the ones we hold in our arms for a moment, but have in our hearts forever.

To the amazing team that brought this book to life:
Andrea, Arlene, Krystina, Tamara, and Debbie.

For every NICU family and caregiver, know that you are never alone.

Family: Alex, Isabelle, Evelyn, & Theodore Ward, Genevieve & Jimmie Hadwyn, Bruce & Judy Immonen, Charles & Maria Immonen, William, Shante, & James Immonen, Monte & Judy Ward, and Quay Ward.

Medical Team: Kathryn Buchan, Mandi Burgamy, Savannah Herzwurm, Tera Howard, Callie O'hear Hutto, Megan and David McCall, Dr. N, Ariel Salas, Kay Windham-Williams.

Beads of Courage®: Beth Moneck and Jean Gribbon
March of Dimes: Shannon Gilbert and David Armstrong
Mothers' Milk Bank at Austin: Kim Updegrove
Medela LLC: Kate Schraml
The Purple Butterfly Project: Nicholas Embleton

Mommy and Daddy were shocked by the news
to find that our blessings were coming in twos.
"What are we having?" we asked through our cries.
Blue bows or pink bows? We liked the surprise!

But early one morning when
something seemed wrong,
to the clinic we raced
unprepared to stay long.

With monitors placed
we found beats of your hearts.
In a snap you were born
just three minutes apart.

One baby, then two -
you both finally had names.
To the NICU you're rushed
there was no one to blame.

Learning to breathe and
to eat on your own,
is a skill that is learned
when a little more grown.

We waited and waited
to see how you'd look,
and Daddy stayed ready
to read you a book.

The days became weeks,
became months to get better.
Some visitors came
bringing gifts and sweet letters.

Through the ups and the downs
Mommy stayed by your sides.
Through the good and the bad
we endured it in strides.

With each passing morning
the stronger you grew.
Then one afternoon
all the nurses just knew.

"It's time to go home!"
said the doctor with praise.
"The stats all look good.
They can leave in three days."

← NICU

Our prayers were answered
and home we did go,
Beads of Courage® in hand
to show all who don't know.

Your time in the NICU
might not move too fast,
but once you are home
it all fades to the past.

So mommies and daddies
of newborns stay strong!
May God bless your journey.
We pray it's not long.

The Story Behind the Story

Alex and Sarah Ward were filled with joy to announce to friends and family that they were pregnant with twins. A few days following their baby shower, the Ward family unexpectedly welcomed their daughters into the world at a gestational age of 28 weeks. The girls were admitted into University of Alabama at Birmingham Hospital's level IV RNICU where they endured a range of life sustaining procedures. After every surgery, test, and therapy they received a bead from the Beads of Courage® program to signify their bravery and provide a tangible medical history of their journey in the NICU. Through the excellent care provided by UAB's medical team and the family's unfailing faith and perseverance, the siblings grew healthier every day. After much uncertainty, the pair was released home 78 days later reuniting their family once again.

Two years later they welcomed their son at 37 weeks, and he was admitted to University Hospital's NICU for a week due to breathing difficulties. The shorter hospital stay did not change the feelings of fear, uncertainty, and disappointment. By grace, all three of the Ward children made it home to grow and thrive. The illustrations include real members of the health teams who helped bring their children home. They pray their story will provide comfort and hope to families who are experiencing, or previously endured, their own NICU journey.

Our NICU Journey is a love letter to children whose beginnings were not what is expected. One in ten babies is born preterm in the United States (March of Dimes.org/peristats; 2019); some of these babies might require treatment in special care units. Many of these fragile infants receive donor milk in their first few days of life to improve their health and increase their chances of survival. Having a newborn admitted to the NICU is never easy and can sometimes be a lengthy endeavor. The Beads of Courage® program provides a visual narrative of NICU stories of courage. For some it ends in victory, but others in tragedy. The family depicted on page 9 is one who lost their son, but was able to take home their daughter. The bear with the purple butterfly represents their lost child who will always hold a place in their hearts. Having a child in the NICU will change you in ways that you never knew. There are many resources out there to help guide you through your journey.

Whatever your story is know that you are not alone.

Resources

For information on joining the Beads of Courage® program please visit www.beadsofcourage.org.

For more information on premature birth and how you can help please visit www.marchofdimes.org.

If you or someone you know would like to donate milk please contact Mothers' Milk Bank at Austin to see if you are eligible and to find your nearest donation center. www.milkbank.org.

Medela is a valuable resource in the NICU and beyond for breastfeeding products and lactation support. For more information visit www.medela.us/breastfeeding.

The Purple Butterfly Project created the symbol of the purple butterfly to signify the loss of a multiple and is dedicated to working with bereaved parents in the NICU. For more information visit www.neonatalbutterflyproject.org.

Love bears all things, believes all things, hopes all things, endures all things.

1 Corinthians 13:7 ESV

Our Journey

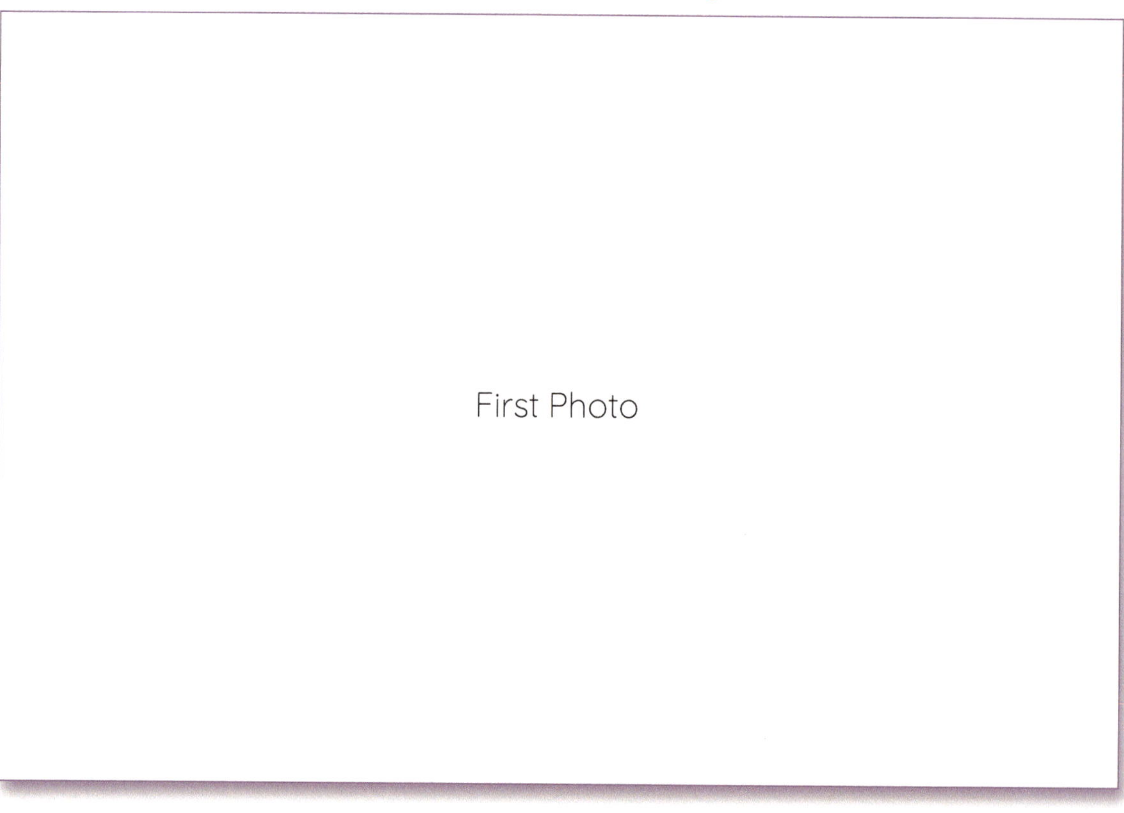

Name(s) ....

Date of Birth ....

Time(s) of Birth ....

Location ....

Birth Weight(s) ....

Length(s) ....

Gestational Age ....

Due Date ....

Discharge Date(s) ....

Days in the NICU ....

NICU Firsts

First Day in the NICU ....

First Surgery ....

First Hold ....

First Kangaroo Care ....

First Day Off Ventilator ....

First Day Off CPAP/Room Air ....

First Day Off Phototherapy ....

First Pacifier ....

First Diaper Change ....

First Outfit ....

First Day at Room Temperature ....

First Day in Open Crib ....

First Bottle ....

First Time Nursing ....

First Bath ....

First Day Without Feeding Tube ....

First Night Rooming In ....

First Time Meeting Family ....

First Time in Car Seat ....

First Night at Home ....

Special Moments: ....

....

....

....

....

....

Guest Signatures

Health Team Signatures

www.ingramcontent.com/pod-product-compliance
Lightning Source LLC
Chambersburg PA
CBHW042050100726
47973CB00014B/208
* 9 7 9 8 9 8 5 1 3 1 2 0 8 *